D1549839

The Power
of Mindfulness

An Inquiry into the Scope of Bare Attention
and the Principal Sources of its Strength

Nyanaponika Thera

Buddhist Publication Society
Kandy—Sri Lanka

Buddhist Publication Society
P.O. Box 61
54, Sangharaja Mawatha
Kandy, Sri Lanka

First published in *The Light of the Dhamma* (Rangoon)

As a Wheel Publication:
First published 1968
Reprinted 1971, 1980, 1986, 1997, 2005, 2011, 2014, 2017

National Library of Sri Lanka—
Cataloguing in Publication Data

Nyanaponika Himi
The Power of Mindfulness / Nyanaponika Himi .- Buddhist Publication Society, 2005
58.; 18 cm.
ISBN 955-24-0002-3
i. 294.34435 DDC 21   ii. Title
1. Buddhist Meditation   2. Buddhism

Typeset in URW Palladio Pali at the BPS

Printed by
Balin Printing Services (Pvt) Ltd.,
Kandy

Contents

Introduction

Is mindfulness actually a power in its own right as claimed by the title of this essay? Seen from the viewpoint of the ordinary pursuits of life, it does not seem so. From that angle mindfulness, or attention, has a rather modest place among many other seemingly more important mental faculties serving the purpose of variegated wish-fulfilment. Here, mindfulness means just "to watch one's steps" so that one may not stumble or miss a chance in the pursuit of one's aims. Only in the case of specific tasks and skills is mindfulness sometimes cultivated more deliberately, but here too it is still regarded as a subservient function, and its wider scope and possibilities are not recognized.

Even if one turns to the Buddha's doctrine, taking only a surface view of the various classifications and lists of mental factors in which mindfulness appears, one may be inclined to regard this faculty just as "one among many." Again one may get the impression that it has a rather subordinate place and is easily surpassed in significance by other faculties.

Mindfulness in fact has, if we may personify it, a rather unassuming character. Compared with it, mental factors such as devotion, energy, imagination and intelligence are certainly more colourful personalities, making an immediate and strong impact on people and situations. Their conquests are sometimes rapid and vast, though often insecure. Mindfulness, on the other hand, is of an unobtrusive nature. Its virtues shine inwardly, and in ordinary life most of its merits are passed on to other mental faculties which generally receive all the credit. One must know mindfulness well and cultivate its acquaintance before one can appreciate its value and its silent penetrative influence. Mindfulness walks slowly and deliberately, and its daily task is of a rather humdrum nature. Yet where it places its feet it cannot easily be dislodged, and it acquires and bestows true mastery of the ground it covers.

Mental faculties of such a nature, like actual personalities of a similar type, are often overlooked or underrated. In the case of mindfulness, it required a genius like the Buddha to discover the "hidden talent" in the modest garb, and to develop the vast inherent power of the potent seed. It is, indeed, the mark of a genius to perceive and to harness the power of the seemingly small. Here, truly, it happens that "what is little becomes much." A revaluation of values takes place. The standards of greatness and smallness change. Through the master mind of the Buddha, mindfulness is finally revealed as the Archimedean point where the vast revolving mass of world suffering is levered out of its twofold anchorage in ignorance and craving.

The Buddha spoke of the power of mindfulness in a very emphatic way:

> "Mindfulness, I declare, is all-helpful." (SN 46:59)

> "All things can be mastered by mindfulness."
>
> (AN 8:83)

Further, there is that solemn and weighty utterance opening and concluding the *Satipaṭṭhāna Sutta*, the *Discourse on the Foundations of Mindfulness*:

> This is the only way, monks, for the purification of beings, for the overcoming of sorrow and lamentation, for the destruction of pain and grief, for reaching the right path, for the attainment of Nibbāna, namely, the four foundations of mindfulness.

In ordinary life, if mindfulness, or attention, is directed to any object, it is rarely sustained long enough for the purpose of careful and factual observation. Generally it is followed immediately by emotional reaction, discriminative thought, reflection or purposeful action. In a life and thought governed by the Buddha's teaching too, mindfulness (*sati*) is mostly linked with clear comprehension (*sampajañña*) of the right purpose or suitability of an action, and other considerations. Thus again it is not viewed in itself. But to tap the actual and potential *power* of mindfulness it is necessary to understand and deliberately cultivate it in its basic, unalloyed form, which we shall call *bare attention*.

By bare attention we understand the clear and single-minded awareness of what actually happens *to* us and *in* us, at the successive moments of perception. It is called "bare" because it attends to the bare facts of a perception without reacting to them by deed, speech or mental comment. Ordinarily, that purely receptive state of mind is, as we said, just a very brief phase of the thought process of which one is often scarcely aware. But in the methodical development of mindfulness aimed at the unfolding of its latent powers, bare attention is sustained for as long a time as one's strength of concentration permits. Bare attention then becomes the key to the meditative practice of Satipaṭṭhāna, opening the door to mind's mastery and final liberation.

Bare attention is developed in two ways: (1) as a methodical meditative practice with selected objects; (2) as applied, as far as practicable, to the normal events of the day, together with a general attitude of mindfulness and clear comprehension. The details of the practice have been described elsewhere, and need not be repeated here.[1]

---

1. See Nyanaponika Thera, *The Heart of Buddhist Meditation* (Kandy, Buddhist Publication Society, 2005).

The primary purpose of this essay is to demonstrate and explain the efficacy of this method, that is, to show the actual *power of mindfulness*. Particularly in an age like ours, with its superstitious worship of ceaseless external activity, there will be those who ask: "How can such a passive attitude of mind as that of bare attention possibly lead to the great results claimed for it?" In reply, one may be inclined to suggest to the questioner that he should not rely on the words of others, but should put these assertions of the Buddha to the test of personal experience. But those who do not yet know the Buddha's teaching well enough to accept it as a reliable guide may hesitate to take up— without good reasons—a practice that, on account of its radical simplicity, may appear strange to them. In the following a number of such "good reasons" are therefore proffered for the reader's scrutiny. They are also meant as an introduction to the general spirit of Satipaṭṭhāna and as pointers to its wide and significant perspectives. Furthermore, it is hoped that one who has taken up the methodical training will recognize in the following observations certain features of his own practice, and be encouraged to cultivate them deliberately.

Four Sources of Power in Bare Attention

We shall now deal with four aspects of bare attention, which are the mainsprings of the power of mindfulness. They are not the only sources of its strength, but they are the principal ones to which its efficacy as a method of mental development is due.

These four are:

1. the functions of "tidying up" and "naming" exercised by bare attention;
2. its non-violent, non-coercive procedure;
3. the capacity of stopping and slowing down;
4. the directness of vision bestowed by bare attention.

1. The Functions of "Tidying" and "Naming"

Tidying Up the Mental Household

If anyone whose mind is not harmonized and controlled through methodical meditative training should take a close look at his own everyday thoughts and activities, he will meet with a rather disconcerting sight. Apart from the few main channels of his purposeful thoughts and activities, he will everywhere be faced with a tangled mass of perceptions, thoughts, feelings and casual bodily movements, showing a disorderliness and confusion which he would certainly not tolerate in his living room. Yet this is the state of affairs that we take for granted within a considerable portion of our waking life and our normal mental activity. Let us now look at the details of that rather untidy picture.

First we meet a vast number of casual sense-impressions such as sights and sounds, passing constantly through our minds. Most of them remain vague and fragmentary; some are even based on faulty perceptions and misjudgements. Carrying these inherent weaknesses, they often form the untested basis for judgements and decisions on a higher level of consciousness. True, all these casual sense-impressions need not and cannot be objects of focused attention. A stone on the road that happens to meet our glance will have a claim on our attention only if it obstructs our progress or is of interest to us for some reason. Yet if we neglect these casual impressions too often, we may stumble over many stones lying on our road and also overlook many gems.

Besides the casual sense impressions, there are those more significant and definite perceptions, thoughts, feelings and volitions, which have a closer connection with our purposeful life. Here too, we find that a very high proportion of them are in a state of utter confusion. Hundreds of cross-currents flash through the mind, and everywhere there are "bits and ends" of unfinished thoughts, stifled emotions and passing moods. Many meet a premature death. Owing to their innately feeble nature, our lack of concentration or their suppression by new and stronger impressions, they do not persist and develop. If we observe our own minds, we shall notice how easily diverted our thoughts are, how often they behave like undisciplined disputants constantly interrupting each other and refusing to listen to the other side's arguments. Again, many lines of thought remain rudimentary or are left untranslated into will and action, because courage is lacking to accept their practical, moral or intellectual consequences. If we continue to examine more closely our average perceptions, thoughts or judgements, we shall have to admit that many of them are unreliable. They are just the products of habit, led by prejudices of intellect or emotion, by our pet preferences or aversions, by faulty or superficial observations, by laziness or by selfishness.

Such a look into long-neglected quarters of the mind will come as a wholesome shock to the observer. It will convince him of the urgent need for methodical mental culture extending below the thin surface layer of the mind to those vast twilight regions of consciousness we have just visited. The observer will then become aware that the relatively small sector of the mind that stands in the intense light of purposeful will and thought is not a reliable standard of the inner strength and lucidity of consciousness in its totality. He will also see that the quality of individual consciousness cannot be judged by a few optimal results of mental activity achieved in brief, intermittent periods. The decisive factor in determining the quality of consciousness is self-understanding and self-control: whether that dim awareness characteristic of our everyday mind and the uncontrolled portion of everyday activity tends to increase or decrease.

It is the daily little negligence in thoughts, words and deeds going on for many years of our lives (and, as the Buddha teaches, for many existences) that is chiefly responsible for the untidiness and confusion we find in our minds. This negligence creates the trouble and allows it to continue. Thus the old Buddhist teachers have said: "Negligence produces a lot of dirt. As in a house, so in the mind, only a very little dirt collects in a day or two, but if it goes on for many years, it will grow into a vast heap of refuse."[1]

---

1. Comy to Sn 334.

The dark, untidy corners of the mind are the hideouts of our most dangerous enemies. From there they attack us unawares, and much too often succeed in defeating us. That twilight world peopled by frustrated desires and suppressed resentments, by vacillations, whims and many other shadowy figures, forms a background from which upsurging passions—greed and lust, hatred and anger—may derive powerful support. Besides, the obscure and obscuring nature of that twilight region is the very element and mother-soil of the third and strongest of the three roots of evil (*akusalamūla*), ignorance or delusion.

Attempts at eliminating the mind's main defilements—greed, hate and delusion—must fail as long as these defilements find refuge and support in the uncontrolled dim regions of the mind; as long as the close and complex tissue of those half-articulate thoughts and emotions forms the basic texture of mind into which just a few golden strands of noble and lucid thought are woven. But how are we to deal with that unwieldy, tangled mass? Usually we try to ignore it and to rely on the counteracting energies of our surface mind. But the only safe remedy is to face it—with mindfulness. Nothing more difficult is needed than to acquire the habit of directing bare attention to these rudimentary thoughts as often as possible. The working principle here is the simple fact that two thoughts cannot exist together at the same time: if the clear light of mindfulness is present, there is no room for mental twilight. When sustained mindfulness has secured a firm foothold, it will be a matter of comparatively secondary importance how the mind will then deal with those rudimentary thoughts, moods and emotions. One may just dismiss them and replace them by purposeful thoughts; or one may allow and even compel them to complete what they have to say. In the latter case they will often reveal how poor and weak they actually are, and it will then not be difficult to dispose of them once they are forced into the open. This procedure of bare attention is very simple and effective; the difficulty is only the persistence in applying it.

Observing a complex thing means identifying its component parts, singling out the separate strands forming that intricate tissue. If this is applied to the complex currents of mental and practical life, automatically a strong regulating influence will be noticeable. As if ashamed in the presence of the calmly observing eye, the course of thoughts will proceed in a less disorderly and wayward manner; it will not be so easily diverted, and will resemble more and more a well-regulated river.

During decades of the present life and throughout millennia of previous lives traversing the round of existence, there has steadily grown within each individual a closely knit system of intellectual and emotional prejudices, of bodily and mental habits that are no longer questioned as to their rightful position and useful function in human life. Here again, the application of bare attention loosens the hard soil of these often very ancient layers of the human mind, preparing thus the ground for sowing the seed of methodical mental training. Bare attention identifies and pursues the single threads of that closely interwoven tissue of our habits. It sorts out carefully the subsequent justifications of passionate impulses and the pretended motives of our prejudices. Fearlessly it questions old habits often grown meaningless. It uncovers their roots, and thus helps abolish all that is seen to be harmful. In brief, bare attention lays open the minute crevices in the seemingly impenetrable structure of unquestioned mental processes. Then the sword of wisdom wielded by the strong arm of constant meditative practice will be able to penetrate these crevices, and finally to break up that structure where required. If the inner connections between the single parts of a seemingly compact whole become intelligible, they then cease to be inaccessible.

When the facts and details of the mind's conditioned nature are uncovered by meditative practice, there is an increased chance to effect fundamental changes in the mind. In that way, not only those hitherto unquestioned habits of the mind, its twilight regions and its normal processes as well, but even those seemingly solid, indisputable facts of the world of matter—all will become "questionable" and lose much of their self-assurance. Many people are so impressed and intimidated by that bland self-assurance of assumed "solid facts," that they hesitate to take up any spiritual training, doubting that it can effect anything worthwhile. The application of bare attention to the task of tidying and regulating the mind will bring perceptible results—results which will dispel their doubts and encourage in them the confidence to enter a spiritual path.

The tidying or regulating function of bare attention, we should note, is of fundamental importance for that "purification of beings" mentioned by the Buddha as the first aim of Satipaṭṭhāna. This phrase refers, of course, to the purification of their minds, and here the very first step is to bring initial order into the functioning of the mental processes. We have seen how this is done by bare attention. In that sense, the commentary to the Discourse on the Foundations of Mindfulness explains the words "for the purification of beings" as follows:

> It is said: "Mental taints defile beings; mental clarity purifies them." That mental clarity comes to be by this way of mindfulness.

Naming

We said before that bare attention "tidies up" or regulates the mind by sorting out and identifying the various confused strands of the mental process. That identifying function, like any other mental activity, is connected with a verbal formulation. In other words, "identifying" proceeds by way of expressly "naming" the respective mental processes.

Primitive man believed that words could exercise a magical power: "Things that could be named had lost their secret power over man, the horror of the unknown. To know the name of a force, a being or an object was (to primitive man) identical with the mastery over it."[1] That ancient belief in the magical potency of names appears also in many fairy tales and myths, where the power of a demon is broken just by facing him courageously and pronouncing his name.

There is an element of truth in the "word-magic" of primitive man, and in the practice of bare attention we shall find the power of naming confirmed. The "twilight demons" of the mind—our passionate impulses and obscure thoughts—cannot bear the simple but clarifying question about their "names," much less the knowledge of these names. Hence this is often alone sufficient to diminish their strength. The calmly observant glance of mindfulness discovers the demons in their hiding-places. The practice of calling them by their names drives them out into the open, into the daylight of consciousness. There they will feel embarrassed and obliged to justify themselves, although at this stage of bare attention they have not yet even been

---

1. Anagarika Govinda, *The Psychological Attitude of Early Buddhist Philosophy* (Rider & Co., 1961).

subjected to any closer questioning except about their names, their identity. If forced into the open while still in an incipient stage, they will be incapable of withstanding scrutiny and will just dwindle away. Thus a first victory over them may be won, even at an early stage of the practice.

The appearance in the mind of undesirable and ignoble thoughts, even if they are very fleeting and only half-articulate, has an unpleasant effect upon one's self-esteem. Therefore such thoughts are often shoved aside, unattended to and unopposed. Often they are also camouflaged by more pleasing and respectable labels which hide their true nature. Thoughts disposed of in either of these two ways will strengthen the accumulated power of ignoble tendencies in the subconscious. Furthermore, these procedures will weaken one's will to resist the arising and the dominance of mental defilements, and strengthen the tendency to evade the issues. But by applying the simple method of clearly and honestly naming or registering any undesirable thoughts, these two harmful devices, ignoring and camouflage, are excluded. Hence their detrimental consequences on the structure of the subconscious and their diversion of mental effort will be avoided.

When ignoble thoughts or personal shortcomings are called by their right names, the mind will develop an inner resistance and even repugnance against them. In time it may well succeed in keeping them in check and finally eliminating them. Even if these means do not bring undesirable tendencies fully under control at once, they will stamp upon them the impact of repeated resistance which will weaken them whenever they reappear. To continue our personification, we may say that unwholesome thoughts will no longer be the unopposed masters of the scene, and this diffidence of theirs will make them considerably easier to deal with. It is the power of moral shame (*hiri-bala*) that has been mustered here as an ally, methodically strengthened by these simple yet subtle psychological techniques.

The method of naming and registering also extends, of course, to noble thoughts and impulses, which will be encouraged and strengthened. Without being given deliberate attention, such wholesome tendencies often pass unnoticed and remain barren. But when clear awareness is applied to them, it will stimulate their growth.

It is one of the most beneficial features of right mindfulness, and particularly of bare attention, that it enables us to utilize all external events and inner mental events for our progress. Even the unsalutary can be made a starting point for the salutary if, through the device of naming or registering, it becomes an object of detached knowledge.

In several passages of the Satipaṭṭhāna Sutta the function of naming or "bare registering" seems to be indicated by formulating the respective statements by way of direct speech. There are no less than four such instances in the discourse:

1. "When experiencing a pleasant feeling, he knows 'I experience a pleasant feeling,'" etc.;
2. "He knows of a lustful (state of) mind, 'Mind is lustful,'" etc.;
3. "If (the hindrance of) sense desire is present in him, he knows, 'Sense desire is present in me,'" etc.;
4. "If the enlightenment factor, mindfulness, is present in him, he knows, 'The enlightenment factor mindfulness is present in me,'" etc.

In concluding this section, we briefly point out that the *tidying up* and the *naming* of mental processes is the indispensable preparation for fully understanding them in their true nature, the task of insight (*vipassanā*). These functions, exercised by bare attention, will help dispel the illusion that the mental processes are compact. They will also help us to discern their specific nature or characteristics and to notice their momentary rise and fall.

2. The Non-coercive Procedure

Obstacles to Meditation

Both the world surrounding us and the world of our own minds are full of hostile and conflicting forces causing us pain and frustration. We know from our own bitter experience that we are not strong enough to meet and conquer all these antagonistic forces in open combat. In the external world we cannot have everything exactly as we want it, while in the inner world of the mind, our passions, impulses and whims often override the demands of duty, reason and our higher aspirations.

We further learn that often an undesirable situation will only worsen if excessive pressure is used against it. Passionate desires may grow in intensity if one tries to silence them by sheer force of will. Disputes and quarrels will go on endlessly and grow fiercer if they are fanned again and again by angry retorts or by vain attempts to crush the other man's position. A disturbance during work, rest or meditation will be felt more strongly and will have a longer-lasting impact if one reacts to it by resentment and anger and attempts to suppress it.

Thus, again and again, we meet with situations in life where we cannot *force* issues. But there are ways of mastering the vicissitudes of life and conflicts of mind without application of force. Non-violent means may often succeed where attempts at coercion, internal or external, fail. Such a non-violent way of mastering life and mind is Satipaṭṭhāna. By the methodical application of bare attention, the basic practice in the development of right mindfulness, all the latent powers of a non-coercive approach will gradually unfold, with their beneficial results and their wide and unexpected implications. In this context we are mainly concerned with the benefits of Satipaṭṭhāna for the mastery of mind, and for the progress in meditation that may result from a non-coercive procedure. But we shall also cast occasional side glances at its repercussions on everyday life. It will not be difficult for a thoughtful reader to make more detailed application to his own problems.

The antagonistic forces that appear in meditation and that are liable to upset its smooth course are of three kinds:

1. external disturbances, such as noise;
2. mental defilements (*kilesa*), such as lust, anger, restlessness, dissatisfaction or sloth, which may arise at any time during meditation; and
3. various incidental stray thoughts, or surrender to day-dreaming.

These distractions are the great stumbling blocks for a beginner in meditation who has not yet acquired sufficient dexterity to deal with them effectively. To give thought to those disturbing factors only when they actually arise at the time of meditation is insufficient. If caught unprepared in one's defence, one will struggle with them in a more or less haphazard and ineffective way, and with a feeling of irritation which will itself be an additional impediment. If disturbances of any kind and unskilful reactions to them occur several times during one session, one may come to feel utterly frustrated and irritated and give up further attempts to meditate, at least for the present occasion.

In fact, even meditators who are quite well informed by books or a teacher about all the details concerning their subject of meditation often lack instruction on how to deal skilfully with the disturbances they may meet. The feeling of helplessness in facing them is the most formidable difficulty for a beginning meditator. At that point many accept defeat, abandoning prematurely any further effort at methodical practice. As in worldly affairs, so in meditation, one's way of dealing with the "initial difficulties" will often be decisive for success or failure.

When faced by inner and outer disturbances, the inexperienced or uninstructed beginner will generally react in two ways. He will first try to shove them away lightly, and if he fails in that, he will try to suppress them by sheer force of will. But these disturbances are like insolent flies: by whisking—first lightly and then with increasing vigour and anger—one may perhaps succeed in driving them away for a while, but usually they will return with an exasperating constancy, and the effort and vexation of whisking will have produced only an additional disturbance of one's composure.

Satipaṭṭhāna, through its method of bare attention, offers a non-violent alternative to those futile and even harmful attempts at suppression by force. A successful non-violent procedure in mind-control has to start with the right attitude. There must be first the full cognizance and sober acceptance of the fact that those three disturbing factors are co-inhabitants of the world we live in, whether we like it or not. Our disapproval of them will not alter the fact. With some we shall have to come to terms, and concerning the others—the mental defilements—we shall have to learn how to deal with them effectively until they are finally conquered.

1. Since we are not the sole inhabitants of this densely populated world, there are bound to be *external disturbances* of various kinds, such as noise and interruptions by visitors. We cannot always live in "splendid isolation," "from noise of men and dogs untroubled," or in "ivory towers" high above the crowd. Right meditation is not escapism; it is not

meant to provide hiding-places for temporary oblivion. Realistic meditation has the purpose of training the mind to face, to understand and to conquer this very world in which we live. And this world inevitably includes numerous obstacles to the life of meditation.

2. The Burmese meditation master, the Venerable Mahāsi Sayādaw, said: "In an unliberated worldling *mental defilements* are sure to arise again and again. He has to face that fact and know these defilements well in order to apply again and again the appropriate remedy of Satipaṭṭhāna. Then they will grow weaker, more short-lived and will finally disappear." To know the occurrence and nature of defilements is therefore as important for a meditator as to know the occurrence of his noble thoughts.

By facing one's own defilements one will be stirred to increase the effort to eliminate them. On the other hand, if out of a false shame or pride one tries to avert one's glance when they arise, one will never truly join issue with them, and will always evade the final and decisive encounter. By hitting blindly at them, one will only exhaust or even hurt oneself. But by observing carefully their nature and behaviour when they arise in one's own mind, one will be able to meet them well prepared, often to forestall them and finally to banish them fully. Therefore meet your defilements with a free and open glance! Be not ashamed, afraid or discouraged!

3. The third group of intruders disturbing the meditator's mind are *stray thoughts* and *daydreams*. These may consist of various memories and images of the past, recent or remote, including those emerging from subconscious depths; thoughts of the future—planning, imagining, fearing, hoping; and the casual sense-perceptions that may occur at the very time of meditation,

often dragging after them a long trail of associated ideas. Whenever concentration and mindfulness slacken, stray thoughts or daydreams appear and fill the vacuum. Though they seem insignificant in themselves, through their frequent occurrence they form a most formidable obstacle, not only for the beginner, but in all cases when the mind is restless or distracted. However, when these invaders can be kept at bay, even long continuous periods of meditation can be achieved. As in the case of the mental defilements, stray thoughts will be entirely excluded only at the stage of Arahatship, when the perfect mindfulness thereby obtained keeps unfailing watch at the door of the mind.

If they are to shape our attitude, all these facts about the three kinds of disturbing factors must be given full weight and be fully absorbed by our minds. Then, in these three disturbing factors, the noble truth of suffering will manifest itself to the meditator very incisively through his own personal experience: "Not to obtain what one wants is suffering." The three other noble truths should also be exemplified by reference to the same situation. In such a way, even when dealing with impediments, the meditator will be within the domain of Satipaṭṭhāna. He will be engaged in the mindful awareness of the Four Noble Truths—part of the contemplation of mental objects (*dhammānupassanā*).[1] It is characteristic of right mindfulness, and one of its tasks, to relate the actual experiences of life to the truths of the Dhamma, and to use them as opportunities for its practical realization. Already at this preliminary stage devoted to the shaping of a correct

---

1.   Bhikkhu Soma, *The Way of Mindfulness* (Kandy: Buddhist Publication Society, 1975), p. 83.

and helpful attitude, we have the first successful test of our peaceful weapons: by understanding our adversaries better, we have consolidated our position, which was formerly weakened by an emotional approach; and by transforming these adversaries into teachers of the truths, we have won the first advantage over them.

Three Countermeasures

If we are mentally prepared by a realistic view of these three factors antagonistic to meditation, we shall be less inclined to react at once with irritation when they actually arise. We shall be emotionally in a better position to meet them with the non-violent weapons of which we shall now speak.

There are three devices for countering disturbances that arise in meditation. The three should be applied in succession whenever the preceding device has failed to dispose of the disturbance. All three are applications of bare attention; they differ in the degree and duration of attention given to the disturbance. The guiding rule here is: to give no more mental emphasis to the respective disturbance than is actually required by circumstances.

1. First, one should notice the disturbance clearly, but lightly: that is, without emphasis and without attention to details. After that brief act of noticing, one should try to return to the original subject of meditation. If the disturbance was weak or one's preceding concentration fairly strong, one may well succeed in resuming contemplation. At that stage, by being careful not to get involved in any "conversation" or argument with the intruder, we shall on our part not give it a reason to stay long; and in a good number of cases the disturbance will soon depart like a visitor who does not receive a very warm

welcome. That curt dismissal may often enable us to return to our original meditation without any serious disturbance to the composure of mind.

The non-violent device here is: to apply bare attention to the disturbance, but with a minimum of response to it, and with a mind bent on withdrawal. This is the very way in which the Buddha himself dealt with inopportune visitors, as described in the *Mahāsuññata Sutta*: … "with a mind bent on seclusion … and withdrawn, his conversation aiming at dismissing (those visitors)." Similar is Śāntideva's advice on how to deal with fools: if one cannot avoid them, one should treat them "with the indifferent politeness of a gentleman."

2. If, however, the disturbance persists, one should repeat the application of bare attention again and again, patiently and calmly; and it may be that the disturbance will vanish when it has spent its force. Here the attitude is to meet the repeated occurrence of a disturbance by a reiterated "No," a determined refusal to be deflected from one's course. This is the attitude of patience and firmness. The capacity for watchful observation has to be aided here by the capacity to wait and to hold one's ground.

These two devices will generally be successful with incidental stray thoughts and daydreams, which are feeble by nature, but the other two types of disturbances, the external ones and defilements, may also yield quite often.

3. But if, for some reason, they do *not* yield, one should deliberately turn one's full attention to the disturbance and make it an object of knowledge. Thus one transforms it from a *disturbance* to meditation into a legitimate *object* of meditation. One may continue with that new object until the external or internal cause for attending to it has ceased; or, if it proves satisfactory, one may even retain it for the rest of that session.

For instance, when disturbed by a persistent noise, we should give the noise our undivided attention, but we should take care to distinguish the object itself from our reaction to it. For example, if resentment arises, it should be clearly recognized in its own nature whenever it arises. In doing so, we shall be practising the contemplation of mind-objects (*dhammānupassanā*) according to the following passage of the Satipaṭṭhāna Sutta: "He knows the ear and sounds, and the fetter (e.g., resentment) arising through both." If the noise is intermittent or of varying intensity, one will easily be able to discern the rise and fall (*udayabbaya*) in its occurrence. In that way one will add to one's direct insight into impermanency (*aniccatā*).

The attitude towards recurrent mental defilements, such as thoughts of lust and restlessness, should be similar. One should face them squarely, but distinguish them from one's reaction to them, e.g., connivance, fear, resentment, irritation. In doing so, one is making use of the device of "naming," and one will reap the benefits mentioned above. In the recurrent waves of passion or restlessness, gradually one will likewise learn to distinguish phases of "high" and "low," their "ups" and "downs," and may also gain other helpful knowledge about their behaviour. By that procedure, one again remains entirely within the range of Satipaṭṭhāna by practising the contemplation of the state of mind (*cittānupassanā*) and of mind-objects (*dhammānu-passanā*: attention to the hindrances).

This method of transforming disturbances to meditation into objects of meditation, as simple as it is ingenious, may be regarded as the culmination of non-violent procedure. It is a device very characteristic of the spirit of Satipaṭṭhāna, to make use of all experiences as aids on the path. In that way enemies are turned into friends; for all these disturbances and antagonistic forces become our teachers, and teachers, whoever they may be, should be regarded as friends.

We cannot forego quoting here a passage from a noteworthy little book, *The Little Locksmith* by Katherine Butler Hathaway, a moving human document of fortitude and practical wisdom acquired by suffering:

> I am shocked by the ignorance and wastefulness with which persons who should know better throw away the things they do not like. They throw away experiences, people, marriages, situations, all sorts of things because they do not like them. If you throw away a thing, it is gone. Where you had something, you have nothing. Your hands are empty; they have nothing to work on. Whereas, almost all those things which get thrown away are capable of being worked over by a little magic into just the opposite of what they were.... But most human beings never remember at all that in almost every bad situation there is the possibility of a transformation by which the undesirable may be changed into the desirable.

We said before that the occurrence of the three disturbing elements cannot always be prevented. They are parts of our world, and their coming and going follow their own laws irrespective of our approval or disapproval. But by applying bare attention we can avoid being swept away or dislodged by them. By taking a firm and calm stand on the secure ground of mindfulness, we shall repeat in a modest degree, but in an essentially identical way, the historic situation under the Bodhi Tree. When Māra the Evil One, at the head of his army, claimed the soil on which the future Buddha sat, the latter refused to budge. Trusting in the power of mindfulness, we may confidently repeat the Bodhisatta's aspiration on that occasion: *Mā maṃ ṭhānā acāvayi* "May he (Māra) not dislodge me from this place" (Padhāna Sutta, Sutta Nipāta).

Let the intruders come and go. Like all the other members of that vast unceasing procession of mental and physical events that passes before our observant eyes in the practice of bare attention, they arise, and having arisen, they pass away.

Our advantage here is the obvious fact that two thought moments cannot be present at the same time. Attention refers, strictly speaking, not to the present but to the moment that has just passed away. Thus, as long as mindfulness holds sway, there will be no "disturbance" or "defiled thought." This gives us the chance to hold on to that secure ground of an "observer's post," our own potential "throne of enlightenment."

By the quietening and neutralizing influence of detached observation as applied in our three devices, the interruptions of meditation will increasingly lose the sting of irritation, and thereby their disturbing effect. This will prove to be an act of true *virāga* (dispassion), which literally means "decolouring." When these experiences are stripped of the emotional tinge that excites towards lust, aversion, irritation and other defilements of the mind, they will appear in their true nature as bare phenomena (*suddha-dhammā*).

The non-violent procedure of bare attention endows the meditator with the light but sure touch so essential for handling the sensitive, evasive and refractory nature of the mind. It also enables him to deal smoothly with the various difficult situations and obstacles met with in daily life. To illustrate the even quality of energy required for attaining to the meditative absorptions, *The Path of Purification*

(*Visuddhimagga*) describes a test which students of surgery in ancient days had to undergo as a proof of their skill. A lotus leaf was placed in a bowl of water, and the pupil had to make an incision through the length of the leaf, without cutting it entirely or submerging it. He who applied an excess of force either cut the leaf into two or pressed it into the water, while the timid one did not even dare to scratch it. In fact, something like the gentle but firm hand of the surgeon is required in mental training, and this skilful, well-balanced touch will be the natural outcome of the non-violent procedure in the practice of bare attention.

3. Stopping and Slowing Down

Keeping Still

For a full and unobstructed unfoldment of the mind's capacities, the influence of two complementary forces is needed: *activating* and *restraining.* That twofold need was recognized by the Buddha, the great knower of mind. He advised that the faculties of energy (*viriy'indriya*) and of concentration (*samādh'indriya*) should be kept equally strong and well balanced.[1] Furthermore, he recommended three of the seven factors of enlightenment (*bojjhaṅga*) as suitable for rousing the mind, and another three for calming it.[2] In both cases, among the spiritual faculties and the enlightenment factors, it is mindfulness that not only watches over their equilibrium, but also activates those that are sluggish and restrains those that are too intense.

Mindfulness, though seemingly of a passive nature, is in fact an activating force. It makes the mind alert, and alertness is indispensable for all purposeful activity. In the present inquiry, however, we shall be mainly concerned with the *restraining* power of mindfulness. We shall examine how it makes for disentanglement and detachment and how it positively helps in the development of the mental qualities required for the work of deliverance.

In practising bare attention, we *keep still* at the mental and spatial place of observation, amidst the loud demands of the inner and outer world. Mindfulness possesses the strength of tranquillity, the capacity for deferring action and

1. See Vism IV.47.
2. Ibid., IV.51, 57. The three rousing factors are investigation, energy and rapture; the three calming ones, tranquillity, concentration and equanimity.

applying the brake, for *stopping* rash interference and for suspending judgement while pausing to observe facts and to reflect upon them wisely. It also brings a wholesome *slowingdown* in the impetuosity of thought, speech and action. Keeping still and stopping, pausing and slowingdown—these will be our key words when speaking now of the restraining effect of bare attention.

An ancient Chinese book states:

In making things end, and in making things start,
there is nothing more glorious than keeping still.

In the light of the Buddha's teaching, the true "end of things" is Nibbāna, which is called the "*stilling* of formations" (*saṅkhārānaṃ vūpasamo*), that is, their final end or cessation. It is also called "the stopping" (*nirodha*). The "things" or "formations" meant here are the conditioned and impersonal phenomena rooted in craving and ignorance. The end of formations comes to be by the end of "forming," that is, by the end of world-creating kammic activities. It is the "end of the world" and of suffering, which the Buddha proclaimed cannot be reached by walking, migrating or transmigrating, but can be found within ourselves. That end of the world is heralded by each deliberate act of *keeping still, stopping or pausing*. "Keeping still," in that highest sense, means stopping the accumulation of kamma, abstaining from our unceasing concern with evanescent things, abstaining from perpetually adding to our entanglements in saṃsāra—the round of repeated birth and death. By following the way of mindfulness, by training ourselves to keep still and pause in the attitude of bare attention, we refuse to take up the world's persistent challenge to our dispositions for greed or hatred. We protect ourselves against rash and delusive judgements; we refrain from blindly plunging into the whirlpool of interfering action with all its inherent dangers.

> He who abstains from interfering is everywhere secure.
> (Sn v. 953)

> He who keeps still and knows where to stop will not meet danger.
> (Tao-Te-Ching, Chapter 44)

The Chinese saying quoted earlier states in its second part that there is nothing more glorious in *making things start* than in keeping still. Explained in the Buddhist sense, these things effectively started by keeping still are "the things (or qualities) making for decrease of kammic accumulation." In dealing with them, we may follow the traditional division of mental training into morality (or conduct), concentration (or tranquillity) and wisdom (or insight). All three are decisively helped by the attitude of *keeping still* cultivated by bare attention.

1. *Conduct*. How can we improve our conduct, its moral quality and its skill in making right decisions? If we earnestly desire such an improvement, it will generally be wisest to choose the line of least resistance. If we turn too quickly against those shortcomings deeply rooted in old habits or in powerful impulses, we might suffer discouraging defeat. We should pay attention first to our blemishes of action and speech and our errors of judgement caused by thoughtlessness and rashness. Of these there are many. In our lives there are numerous instances where one short moment of reflection might have prevented a false step, and thereby warded off a long chain of misery or moral guilt that started with a single moment of thoughtlessness. But how can we curb our rash reactions, and replace them with moments of mindfulness and

reflection? To do so will depend on our capacity to *stop and pause*, to apply the brakes at the right time, and this we can learn by practising bare attention. In that practice we shall train ourselves "to look and wait," to suspend reactions or slow them down. We shall learn it first the easy way, in situations of our own choice, within the limited field of experiences met with during the periods of meditative practice. When facing again and again the incidental sense impressions, feelings or stray thoughts which interrupt our concentration; when curbing again and again our desire to respond to them in some way; when succeeding again and again in keeping still in face of them—we shall be preparing ourselves to preserve that inner stillness in the wider and unprotected field of everyday life. We shall have acquired a presence of mind that will enable us to pause and stop, even if we are taken by surprise or are suddenly provoked or tempted.

Our present remarks refer to those blemishes of conduct liable to arise through thoughtlessness and rashness, but which may be more or less easily checked through mindfulness. Dexterity in dealing with these will also affect those more obstinate deviations from moral conduct rooted in strong passionate impulses or in deeply ingrained bad habits. The increased tranquillity of mind achieved in keeping still for bare attention will restrain the impetuosity of passions. The acquired habit of pausing and stopping will act as a brake to the ingrained habits of indulging in unwholesome deeds.

By being able to keep still for bare attention, or to pause for wise reflection, very often the first temptation to lust, the first wave of anger, the first mist of delusion, will disappear without causing serious entanglement. At which point the current of unwholesome thought processes is stopped will depend on the quality of mindfulness. If mindfulness is keen, it will succeed at a very early point in calling a stop to a series of defiled thoughts or actions before we are carried along by them too far. Then the respective defilements will not grow beyond their initial strength, less effort will be required to check them and fewer kammic entanglements, or none, will follow.

Let us take the example of a pleasant visual object that has aroused our liking. At first that liking might not be very active and insistent. If at this point the mind is already able to keep still for detached observation or reflection, the visual perception can easily be divested of its still very slight admixture of lust. The object becomes registered as "just something seen that has caused a pleasant feeling," or the attraction felt is sublimated into a quiet aesthetic pleasure. But if that earliest chance has been missed, the liking will grow into attachment and into the desire to possess. If now a stop is called, the thought of desire may gradually lose its strength; it will not easily turn into an insistent craving, and no actual attempts to get possession of the desired object will follow. But if the current of lust is still unchecked, then the thought of desire may express itself by speech in asking for the object or even demanding it with impetuous words. That is, unwholesome mental kamma is followed by unwholesome verbal kamma. A refusal will cause the original current of lust to branch out into additional streams of mental defilements, either sadness or anger. But if even at that late stage one can stop for quiet reflection or bare attention, accept the refusal and renounce wish-fulfilment, further complications will be avoided. However, if clamouring words are followed by unwholesome bodily kamma, and if, driven by craving, one tries to get possession of the desired object by stealth or force, then the kammic entanglement is complete and its consequences must be experienced in their full impact. But still, if even after the completion of the evil act, one stops for reflection, it will not be in vain. For the mindfulness that arises in the form of remorseful retrospection will preclude a hardening of character and may prevent a repetition of the same action. The Exalted One once said to his son, Rāhula:

> Whatever action you *intend* to perform, by body, speech or mind, you should consider that action.... If, in considering it, you realize: "This action which I intend to perform will be harmful to myself, or harmful to others, or harmful to both; it will be an unwholesome action, producing suffering, resulting in suffering"—then you should certainly not perform that action.
>
> Also *while* you are performing an action, by body, speech or mind, you should consider that action.... If, in considering it, you realize: "This action which I am performing is harmful to myself, or harmful to others, or harmful to both; it is an unwholesome action, producing suffering, resulting in suffering"—then you should desist from such an action.
>
> Also *after* you have performed an action, by body, speech or mind, you should consider that action.... If, in considering it, you realize: "This action which I have performed has been harmful to myself, to others, or harmful to both; it was an unwholesome action producing suffering, resulting in suffering"—then you should in future refrain from it. (MN 61)

2. *Tranquillity.* We shall now consider how stopping for bare attention also helps one to attain and strengthen tranquillity (*samatha*) in its double sense: general peace of mind and meditative concentration.

By developing the habit of pausing for bare attention, it becomes increasingly easier to withdraw into one's own inner stillness when unable to escape bodily from the loud, insistent noises of the outer world. It will be easier to forego useless reactions to the foolish speech or deeds of others. When the blows of fate are particularly hard and incessant, a mind trained in bare attention will find a refuge in the haven of apparent passivity or watchful non-action, from which position it will be able to wait patiently until the storms have passed. There are situations in life when it is best to allow things to come to their natural end. He who is able to keep still and wait will often succeed where aggressiveness or busy activity would fail. Not only in critical situations, but also in the normal course of life, the experience won by observant keeping still will convince us that we need not actively respond to every impression we receive, or regard every encounter with people or things as a challenge to our interfering activity.

By refraining from busying ourselves unnecessarily, external frictions will be reduced and the internal tensions they bring will loosen up. Greater harmony and peace will pervade the life of every day, bridging the gap between normal life and the tranquillity of meditation. Then there will be fewer of those disturbing inner reverberations of everyday restlessness which, in a coarse or subtle form, invade the hours of meditation, producing bodily and mental unrest. Consequently, the hindrance of agitation, a chief obstacle to concentration, will appear less often and will be easier to overcome when it arises.

By cultivating the attitude of bare attention as often as opportunity offers, the centrifugal forces of mind, making for mental distraction, will peter out; the centripetal tendency, turning the mind inward and making for concentration, will gather strength. Craving will no longer run in pursuit of a variety of changing objects.

Regular practice of sustained attention to a continuous series of events prepares the mind for sustained concentration on a *single* object, or a limited number of objects, in the strict practice of meditation. Firmness or steadiness of mind, another important factor in concentration, will likewise be cultivated.

Thus, the practice of keeping still, pausing and stopping for bare attention, fosters several salient components of meditative tranquillity: calmness, concentration, firmness and reduction of the multiplicity of objects. It raises the average level of normal consciousness and brings it closer to the level of the meditative mind. This is an important point because often too wide a gap between these two mental levels repeatedly frustrates attempts at mental concentration and hinders the achievement of smooth continuity in meditative practice.

In the sequence of the seven factors of enlightenment, we find that the enlightenment factor of tranquillity (*passaddhi-sambojjhaṅga*) precedes that of concentration (*samādhi-sambojjhaṅga*). Expressing the same fact, the Buddha says: "If tranquillized within, the mind will become concentrated." Now in the light of our previous remarks, we shall better understand these statements.

3. *Insight*. It has been said by the Exalted One: "He whose mind is concentrated sees things as they really are." Therefore, all those ways by which bare attention strengthens concentration also provide a supporting condition for the development of insight. But there is also a more direct and specific help which insight receives from keeping still in bare attention.

Generally, we are more concerned with handling and using things than with knowing them in their true nature. Thus we usually grasp in haste the very first few signals conveyed to us by a perception. Then, through deeply ingrained habit, those signals evoke a standard response by way of judgements such as good-bad, pleasant-unpleasant, useful-harmful, right-wrong. These judgements, by which we define the objects in relation to ourselves, lead to corresponding reactions by word or deed. Only rarely does attention dwell upon a common or familiar object for any longer time than is needed to receive the first few signals. So, for the most part, we perceive things in a fragmentary manner and thus misconceive them. Further, only the very first phase of the object's life-span, or a little more, comes into the focus of our attention. One may not even be consciously aware that the object is a process with an extension in time—a beginning and an end; that it has many aspects and relations beyond those casually perceived in a limited situation; that, in brief, it has a kind of evanescent individuality of its own.

A world perceived in this superficial way will consist of shapeless little lumps of experiences marked by a few subjectively selected signs or symbols. The symbols chosen are determined mainly by the individual's self-interest; sometimes they are even misapplied. The shadow-like world that results includes not only the outer environment and other persons, but also a good part of one's own bodily and mental processes. These, too, become subjected to the same superficial manner of conceptualization.

The Buddha points out four basic misconceptions that result from distorted perceptions and unmethodical attention: taking the impure for pure, the impermanent for lasting, the painful and pain-bringing for pleasant and the impersonal for a self or something belonging to the self. When the seal of self-reference is thus stamped again and again upon the world of everyday experience, the basic misconception, "This belongs to me" (*attaniya*) will steadily put forth roots into all the bodily and mental factors of our being. Like the hair-roots of a plant, these will be fine, but firm and widespread—to such an extent, in fact, that the notions of "I" and "mine" will hardly be shaken by merely intellectual convictions about the non-existence of a self (*anattā*).

These grave consequences issue from the fundamental perceptual situation: our rush into hasty or habitual reactions after receiving the first few signals from our perceptions. But if we muster the restraining forces of mindfulness and pause for bare attention, the material and mental processes that form the objects of mind at the given moment will reveal themselves to us more fully and more truly. No longer dragged at once into the whirlpool of self-reference, allowed to unfold themselves before the watchful eye of mindfulness, they will disclose the diversity of their aspects and the wide net of their correlations and interconnections. The connection with self-interest, so narrow and often falsifying, will recede into the background, dwarfed by the wider view now gained. The processes observed display in their serial occurrence and in their component parts a constant birth and death, a rise and a fall. Thereby the facts of change and impermanence impress themselves on the mind with growing intensity.

The same discernment of rise and fall dissolves the false conceptions of unity created under the influence of the egocentric attitude. Self-reference uncritically overrides diversity; it lumps things together under the preconceptions of *being* a self or *belonging* to a self. But bare attention reveals these sham unities as impersonal and conditioned phenomena. Facing thus again and again the evanescent, dependent and impersonal nature of life-processes within and without, we shall discover their monotony and unsatisfactory nature: in other words, the truth of suffering. Thus, by the simple device of slowing down, pausing and keeping still for bare attention, all three of the characteristics of existence—impermanence, suffering and non-self—will open themselves to penetrative insight (*vipassanā*).

Spontaneity

An acquired or strengthened habit of pausing mindfully before acting does not exclude a wholesome spontaneity of response. On the contrary, through training, the practice of pausing, stopping and keeping still for bare attention will itself become quite spontaneous. It will grow into a selective mechanism of the mind that, with an increasing reliability and swiftness of response, can prevent the upsurge of evil or unwise impulses. Without such a skill we may intellectually realize those impulses to be unwholesome, but still succumb to them owing to their own powerful spontaneity. The practice of pausing mindfully serves, therefore, to replace unwholesome spontaneity or habits with wholesome ones grounded in our better knowledge and nobler intentions.

Just as certain reflex movements automatically protect the body, similarly the mind needs spontaneous spiritual and moral self-protection. The practice of bare attention will provide this vital function. A person of average moral standards instinctively shrinks from thoughts of theft or murder. With the help of the method of bare attention, the range of such spontaneous moral brakes can be vastly extended and ethical sensitivity greatly heightened.

In an untrained mind, noble tendencies and right thoughts are often assailed by the sudden outbreak of passions and prejudices. They either succumb or assert themselves only with difficulty after an inner struggle. But if the spontaneity of the unwholesome is checked or greatly reduced, as described above, our good impulses and wise reflections will have greater scope to emerge and express themselves freely and spontaneously. Their natural flow will give us greater confidence in the power of the good within us; it will also carry more conviction for others. That spontaneity of the good will not be erratic, for it will have deep and firm roots in previous methodical training. Here appears a way by which a premeditated good thought (*sasaṅkhārika-kusala-citta*) may be transformed into a spontaneous good thought (*asaṅkhārika-kusala-citta*). According to the psychology of the Abhidhamma Piṭaka, such a thought, if combined with knowledge, takes the first place in the scale of ethical values. In this way we shall achieve a practical understanding of a saying in *The Secret of the Golden Flower*:[1] "If one attains intentionally to an unintentional state one has comprehension." This saying invites a paraphrase in Pali terms: *Sasaṅkhārena asaṅkhārikaṃ pattabbaṃ*, "By premeditated intentional effort spontaneity can be won."

If the numerous aids to mental growth and liberation found in the Buddha's teachings are wisely utilized, there is actually nothing that can finally withstand the Satipaṭṭhāna method; and this method starts with the simple practice of learning to pause and stop for bare attention.

---

1. A treatise of Chinese Taoism, strongly influenced by Mahāyāna Buddhism.

Slowing Down

Against the impetuosity, rashness and heedlessness of the untrained mind, the practice of pausing and stopping sets up a deliberate slowing down. The demands of modern life, however, make it impracticable to introduce such a slowing-down of functions into the routine of the average working day. But as an antidote against the harmful consequences of the hectic speed of modern life, it is all the more important to cultivate that practice in one's leisure hours, especially in periods of strict Satipaṭṭhāna practice. Such practice will also bestow the worldly benefits of greater calm, efficiency and skill in one's daily round of work.

For the purposes of meditative development, slowing-down serves as an effective training in heedfulness, sense-control and concentration. But apart from that, it has a more specific significance for meditative practice. In the commentary to the *Satipaṭṭhāna Sutta*, it is said that the slowing down of movements may help in *regaining lost concentration* on a chosen object. A monk, so we read, had bent his arm quickly without remembering his subject of meditation as his rule of practice demanded. On becoming aware of that omission he took his arm back to its previous position and repeated the movement mindfully. The subject of meditation referred to was probably "clearly compre-hending action," as mentioned in the *Satipaṭṭhāna Sutta*: "In bending and stretching he acts with clear comprehension."

The slowing-down of certain bodily movements during strict meditative training is particularly helpful in gaining *insight-knowledge* (*vipassanā-ñāṇa*), especially the direct awareness of change and non-self. To a great extent, it is the rapidity of movement that strengthens the illusion of unity, identity and substantiality in what is actually a complex evanescent process. Therefore, in the strict practice of

Satipaṭṭhāna, the slowing down of such actions as walking, bending and stretching, so as to discern the several phases of each movement, provides a powerful aid for direct insight into the three characteristics of all phenomena. The meditator's contemplation will gain increasing force and significance if he notices clearly how each partial phase of the process observed arises and ceases by itself, and nothing of it goes over or "transmigrates" to the next phase.

Under the influence of pausing for bare attention, the average rhythm of our everyday actions, speech and thoughts will also become more quiet and peaceful. Slowing-down the hurried rhythm of life means that thoughts, feelings and perceptions will be able to complete the entire length of their natural lifetime. Full awareness will extend up to their end phase: to their last vibrations and reverberations. Too often that end phase is cut off by an impatient grasping at new impressions, or by hurrying on to the next stage of a line of thought before the earlier one has been clearly comprehended. This is one of the main reasons for the disorderly state of the average mind, which is burdened by a vast amount of indistinct or fragmentary perceptions, stunted emotions and undigested ideas. Slowing-down will prove an effective device for recovering the fullness and clarity of consciousness. A fitting simile, and at the same time an actual example, is the procedure called for in the practice of mindfulness of breathing (*ānāpānasati*): mindfulness has to cover the whole extent of the breath, its beginning, middle and end. This is what is meant by the passage in the sutta, "Experiencing the *whole* (breath) body, I shall breathe in and out." Similarly, the entire "breath" or rhythm of our lives will become deeper and fuller if, through slowing-down, we get used to sustained attention.

The habit of prematurely cutting off processes of thought, or slurring over them, has assumed serious proportions in the man of modern urban civilization. Restlessly he clamours for ever new stimuli in increasingly quicker succession, just as he demands increasing speed in his means of locomotion. This rapid bombardment of impressions has gradually blunted his sensitivity, and thus he always needs new stimuli, louder, coarser and more variegated. Such a process, if not checked, can end only in disaster. Already we see at large a decline of finer aesthetic susceptibility and a growing incapacity for genuine natural joy. The place of both is taken by a hectic, short-breathed excitement incapable of giving any true aesthetic or emotional satisfaction. "Shallow mental breath" is to a great extent responsible for the growing superficiality of "civilized man" and for the frightening spread of nervous disorders in the West. It may well become the start of a general deterioration of human consciousness in its qualitative level, range and strength. This danger threatens all those, in the East as well as in the West, who lack adequate spiritual protection from the impact of technical civilization. Satipaṭṭhāna can make an important contribution to remedying this situation, in the way we have briefly indicated here. Thus the method will prove beneficial from the worldly point of view as well.

Here, however, we are chiefly concerned with the psychological aspects of mindfulness and their significance for meditative development. Sustained attention, helped by slowing-down, will affect the quality of consciousness mainly in three ways: (a) in intensifying consciousness; (b) in clarifying the object's characteristic features; and (c) in revealing the object's relatedness.

(a) An object of sustained attention will exert a particularly *strong* and *long-lasting* impact on the mind. Its influence will be felt not only throughout the thought-series immediately following the particular perception, but may also extend far into the future. It is that causal efficacy which is the measure of the *intensity of consciousness*.

(b) Sustained attention leads to a *fuller picture* of the object in all its aspects. Generally, the first impression we gain of any new sense-object or idea will be its most striking feature; it is this aspect of the object which captures our attention up to the culminating point of the impact. But the object also displays other aspects or characteristics, and is capable of exercising functions other than those we initially notice. These may be less obvious to us or subjectively less interesting; but they may be even more important. There will also be cases where our first impression is entirely deceptive. Only if we sustain our attention beyond that first impact will the object reveal itself more fully. In the downward course of the first perceptual wave the prejudicing force of the first impact lessens; and it is only then, in that end phase, that the object will yield a wider range of detail, a more complete picture of itself. It is therefore only by sustained attention that we can obtain a *clearer understanding of an object's characteristic features*.

(c) Among the characteristic features of any object, physical or mental, there is one class we often overlook due to hasty or superficial attention, and which therefore needs to be treated separately. This is the *relatedness* of the object. The object's relatedness extends back to its past—to its origin, causes, reasons and logical precedents; it also extends outward to embrace the total context—its background, environment and presently active influences. We can never fully understand things if we view them in artificial isolation. We have to see them as part of a wider pattern, in their conditioned and conditioning nature; and this can be done only with the help of sustained attention.

Subliminal Influences

The three ways of heightening consciousness just discussed are clearly of prime importance for the development of insight. When consciousness is intensified, and its objective field clarified and discerned in its relational structure, the ground is prepared for "seeing things according to reality." But besides its obvious direct influence, this threefold process also has an indirect influence which is no less powerful and important: it strengthens and sharpens the mind's subliminal faculties of subconscious organization, memory and intuition. These again, on their part, nourish and consolidate the progress of liberating insight. The insight aided by them is like the mountain lake of the canonical simile: it is fed not only by the outside rains, but also by springs welling up from within its own depths. The insight nourished by these "underground" subliminal resources of the mind will have deep roots. The meditative results that it brings cannot be lost easily, even with unliberated worldlings who are still subject to relapse.

1. Perceptions or thoughts which have been objects of sustained attention make a stronger impact on the mind and reveal their characteristic features more distinctly than when attention is slack. Thus, when they sink into the subconscious, they occupy a special position there. This holds true for all three ways of enhancing the consciousness of an object. (a) In a process of consciousness, if attention is as strong in the end phase as in the earlier phases, then when the process is finished and the mind lapses back into subconsciousness, the latter will be more amenable to

conscious control. (b) If an impression or idea has been marked by numerous distinct characteristics, then when it fades from immediate awareness, it will not be so easily lost in the vague contents of the subconscious or dragged by passionate biases into false subconscious associations. (c) Similarly, the correct comprehension of the object's relatedness will protect the experience from being merged with indistinct subconscious material. Perceptions or thoughts of enhanced intensity and clarity, absorbed into the subconscious, remain more articulate and more accessible than contents originating from hazy or "stunned" impressions. It will be easier to convert them into full consciousness and they will be less unaccountable in their hidden effects upon the mind. If, through an improvement in the quality and range of mindfulness, the number of such matured impressions increases, the result might be a subtle change in the very structure of subconsciousness itself.

2. It will be evident from our earlier remarks that those impressions that we have called "matured" or "more accessible and convertible" lend themselves more easily and more correctly to recollection—more easily because of their greater intensity, more correctly because their clearly marked features protect them from being distorted by false associative images or ideas. Remembering them in their context and relatedness works both ways—it promotes both easier and more correct recollection. Thus *sati* in its meaning and function of mindfulness helps to strengthen *sati* in its meaning and function of *memory.*

3. The influence of sustained attention on the subconscious and on memory brings a deepening and strengthening of the faculty of intuition, particularly the intuitive insight which chiefly concerns us here. Intuition is

not a gift from the unknown. Like any other mental faculty, it arises out of specific conditions. In this case the primary conditions are latent memories of perceptions and thoughts stored in the subconscious. Obviously, the memories providing the most fertile soil for the growth of intuition will be those marked by greater intensity, clarity and wealth of distinctive marks; for it is these that are most accessible. Here, too, the preserved relatedness of the impressions will contribute much. Recollections of that type will have a more organic character than memories of bare or vague isolated facts, and they will fall more easily into new patterns of meaning and significance. These more articulate memory images will be a strong stimulation and aid for the intuitive faculty. Silently, in the hidden depths of the subliminal mind, the work of collecting and organizing the subconscious material of experience and knowledge goes on until it is ripe to emerge as an *intuition*. The breakthrough of that intuition is sometimes occasioned by quite ordinary happenings. However, though seemingly ordinary, these events may have a strong evocative power if previously they had been made objects of sustained attention. Slowing-down and pausing for bare attention will uncover the depth dimension of the simple things of everyday life, and thus provide potential stimuli for the intuitive faculty.

This applies also to the intuitive penetration of the Four Noble Truths that culminates in liberation (*arahatta*). The scriptures record many instances of monks and nuns who could not arrive at intuitive penetration when engaged in the actual practice of insight meditation. The flash of intuition struck them on quite different occasions: when stumbling against a rock or catching sight of a forest fire, a mirage or a lump of froth in a river. We meet here another confirmation of that seemingly paradoxical saying that "intentionally an unintentional state may be won." By deliberately turning the full light of mindfulness on the smallest events and actions of everyday life, eventually the liberating wisdom may arise.

Sustained attention not only provides the nourishing soil for the *growth* of intuition, it also makes possible the fuller utilization and even repetition of the intuitive moment. People of inspiration in various fields of creative activity have often deplored their common experience: the flash of intuition strikes so suddenly and vanishes so quickly that frequently the slow response of the mind hardly catches the last glimpse of it. But if the mind has been trained in observant pausing, in slowing-down and sustained attention, and if—as indicated above—the subconscious has been influenced, then the intuitive moment too might gain that fuller, slower and stronger rhythm. This being the case, its impact will be strong and clear enough to allow for full use of that flash of intuitive insight. It might even be possible to lead its fading vibrations upward again to a new culmination, similar to the rhythmic repetition of a melody rising again in harmonious development out of the last notes of its first appearance.

The full utilization of a single moment of intuitive insight could be of decisive importance for one's progress towards full realization. If one's mental grip is too weak and one lets those elusive moments of intuitive insight slip away without having utilized them fully for the work of liberation, then they might not recur until many years have passed, or perhaps not at all during the present life. Skill in sustained attention, however, will allow one to make full use of such opportunities, and slowing-down and pausing during meditative practice is an important aid in acquiring that skill.

Through our treatment of pausing, stopping and slowing-down, one of the traditional definitions of mindfulness found in the Pali scriptures will have become more intelligible in its far-reaching implications: that is, its function of *anapilāpanatā*, meaning literally, "not floating (or slipping) away." "Like pumpkin-pots on the surface of water," add the commentators, and they continue: "Mindfulness enters deeply into its object, instead of hurrying only over its surface." Therefore, "non-superficiality" will be an appropriate rendering of the above Pali term, and a fitting characterization of mindfulness.

4. Directness of Vision

I wish I could disaccustom myself from everything, so
that I might see anew, hear anew, feel anew. Habit
spoils our philosophy.

G.C. Lichtenberg (1742–1799)

In an earlier section we spoke about the impulsive
spontaneity of the unwholesome. We have seen how
stopping for bare and sustained attention is able to counter,
or reduce, our rash impulsive reactions, thus allowing us to
face any situation with a fresh mind, with a *directness of
vision* unprejudiced by those first spontaneous responses.

By *directness of vision* we understand a direct view of
reality, without any colouring or distorting lenses, without
the intrusion of emotional or habitual prejudices and
intellectual biases. It means: coming face to face with the
bare facts of actuality, seeing them as vividly and freshly as
if we were seeing them for the first time.

The Force of Habit

Those spontaneous reactions which so often stand in the
way of direct vision do not derive only from our passionate
impulses. Very frequently they are the product of *habit*. In
that form, they generally have an even stronger and more
tenacious hold on us—a hold which may work out either
for our good or for our harm. The influence that habit
exercises for the *good* is seen in the "power of repeated
practice." This power protects our achievements and
skills—whether manual or mental, worldly or spiritual—
against loss or forgetfulness, and converts them from
casual, short-lived imperfect acquisitions into the more
secure possession of a quality thoroughly mastered. The

detrimental effect of habitual spontaneous reactions is manifest in what is called in a derogative sense the "force of habit": its deadening, stultifying and narrowing influence productive of compulsive behaviour of various kinds. In our present context we shall be concerned only with that negative aspect of habit as impeding and obscuring the directness of vision.

As remarked earlier, habitual reactions generally have a stronger influence upon our behaviour than impulsive ones. Our passionate impulses may disappear as suddenly as they have arisen. Though their consequences may be very grave and extend far into the future, their influence is in no way as long-lasting and deep-reaching as that of habit. Habit spreads its vast and closely meshed net over wide areas of our life and thought, trying to drag in more and more. Our passionate impulses, too, might be caught in that net and thus be transformed from passing outbursts into lasting traits of character. A momentary impulse, an occasional indulgence, a passing whim may by repetition become a habit we find difficult to uproot, a desire hard to control and finally an automatic function we no longer question. Repeated gratification turns a desire into a habit, and a habit left unchecked grows into a compulsion.

It sometimes happens that, at first, we regard a particular activity or mental attitude as without any special personal importance. The activity or attitude may be morally indifferent and inconsequential. At the start we might find it easy to abandon it or even to exchange it for its opposite, since neither our emotions nor reason bias us towards either alternative. But by repetition, we come to regard the chosen course of action or thought as "pleasant, desirable and correct," even as "righteous"; and thus we finally identify it with our character or personality. Consequently, we feel any break in this routine to be unpleasant or wrong. Any outside interference with it we greatly resent, even regarding such interference as a threat to our "vital interests and principles." In fact at all times primitive minds, whether "civilized" or not, have looked at a stranger with his "strange customs" as an enemy, and have felt his mere unaggressive presence as a challenge or threat.

At the beginning, when no great importance was ascribed to the specific habit, the attachment that gradually formed was directed not so much to the action proper as to the pleasure we derived from undisturbed routine. The strength of that attachment to routine derives partly from the force of physical and mental inertia, so powerful a motive in man; we shall presently refer to another cause for attachment to routine. By force of habit, the particular concern—whether a material object, an activity or a way of thinking—comes to be invested with such an increase of emotional emphasis, that the attachment to quite unimportant or banal things may become as tenacious as that to our more fundamental needs. Thus the lack of conscious control can turn the smallest habits into the uncontested masters of our lives. It bestows upon them the dangerous power to limit and rigidify our character and to narrow our freedom of movement—environmental, intellectual and spiritual. Through our subservience to habit, we forge new fetters for ourselves and make ourselves vulnerable to new attachments, aversions, prejudices and predilections; that is, to new suffering. The danger for spiritual development posed by the dominating influence of habit is perhaps more serious today than ever before; for the expansion of habit is particularly noticeable in our present age when specialization and standardization reach into so many varied spheres of life and thought.

Therefore, when considering the Satipaṭṭhāna Sutta's words on the formation of fetters, we should also think of the important part played by habit:

> ... and what fetter arises dependent on both (i.e., the sense organs and sense objects), that he knows well. In what manner the arising of the unarisen fetter comes to be, that he knows well.

In Buddhist terms, it is pre-eminently the hindrance of sloth and torpor (*thīna-middha-nīvaraṇa*) that is strengthened by the force of habit, and it is the mental faculties such as agility and pliancy of mind (*kāya-* and *citta-lahutā*, etc.)[1] that are weakened.

This tendency of habits to extend their range is anchored in the very nature of consciousness. It stems not only from the aforementioned passive force of inertia, but in many cases from an active will to dominate and conquer. Certain active types of consciousness, possessing a fair degree of intensity, tend to repeat themselves. Each one struggles to gain ascendancy, to become a centre around which other weaker mental and physical states revolve, adapting themselves to and serving that central disposition. This tendency is never quite undisputed, but still it prevails, and even peripheral or subordinate types of consciousness exhibit the same urge for ascendancy. This is a striking parallel to the self-assertion and domineering tendency of an egocentric individual in his contact with society. Among biological analogies, we may mention the tendency towards expansion shown by cancer and other pathological growths; the tendency towards repetition we meet in the

---

1.   About these important qualitative constituents of good, wholesome (*kusala*) consciousness, see the author's *Abhidhamma Studies* (Kandy: Buddhist Publication Society, 1965), pp. 51 ff.

freak mutations which loom as a grave danger at the horizon of our atomic age.

Because of that will to dominate inherent in many types of consciousness, a passing whim may grow into a relatively constant trait of character. If still not satisfied with its position, it may break away entirely from the present combination of life forces until finally, in the process of rebirths, it becomes the very centre of a new personality. There are within us countless seeds for new lives, for innumerable potential "beings," all of whom we should vow to liberate from the wheel of saṃsāra, as the Sixth Zen Patriarch expressed it.[1]

Detrimental physical or mental habits may grow strong, not only if fostered deliberately, but also if left unnoticed or unopposed. Much of what has now strong roots in our nature has grown from minute seeds planted in a long-forgotten past (see the Simile of the Creeper, MN 45). This growth of morally bad or otherwise detrimental habits can be effectively checked by gradually developing another habit: that of attending to them mindfully. If we now do deliberately what had become a mechanical performance, and if prior to doing it we pause a while for bare attention and reflection—this will give us a chance to scrutinize the habit and clearly comprehend its purpose and suitability (*sātthaka-* and *sappāya-sampajañña*). It will allow us to make a fresh assessment of the situation, to see it directly, unobscured by the mental haze that surrounds a habitual activity with the false assurance: "It is right because it was

---

1. This may be a somewhat ironical reference by that great sage to the fact that the well-known Mahāyānic Bodhisattva vow of liberating all beings of the universe is often taken much too light-heartedly by many of his fellow Mahāyānists.

done before." Even if a detrimental habit cannot be broken quickly, the reflective pause will counter its unquestioned spontaneity of occurrence. It will stamp it with the seal of repeated scrutiny and resistance, so that on its recurrence it will be weaker and will prove more amenable to our attempts to change or abolish it.

It need hardly be mentioned that habit, which has been rightly called "the wet-nurse of man," cannot and should not disappear from our lives. Let us only remember what a relief it is, particularly in the crowded day and complex life of a city-dweller, to be able to do a great number of things fairly mechanically with, as it were, only "half-powered attention." Habit brings considerable simplification to our lives. It would be an unbearable strain if all our little humdrum activities had to be done with deliberate effort and close attention. In fact, many operations of manual labour, much of the *technique* in art, and even standard procedures in complex intellectual work, generally bring better and more even results through skilled routine performance. Yet that evenness of habitual performance will also reach its end point. Unless enlivened by the creation of new interest, it will show symptoms of fatigue and start to decline.

Of course it would be absurd to advocate that all our little habits be abolished, for many are innocuous and even useful. But we should regularly ask ourselves whether we still have control over them; whether we can give them up or alter them at will. We can answer this question for ourselves in two ways: first, by attending to our habitual actions mindfully for a certain period of time, and second, by actually giving them up temporarily in cases where this will not have any harmful or disturbing effects upon ourselves or others. If we turn on them the light of *direct vision*, looking at them or performing them as if for the first time, these little routine activities, and the habitual sights around us, will assume a new glow of interest and stimulation. This also holds good for our professional occupations and their environment, and for our close human relationships if they should have become stale by habit. The relationship to one's marriage partner, to friends and to colleagues may thus receive a great rejuvenation. A fresh and direct vision will also reveal that one can relate to people or do things in a different and more beneficial way than one did before by force of habit.

An acquired capacity to give up minor habits will prove its worth in the fight against more dangerous proclivities. It will also come to our aid at times when we are faced with serious changes in our lives which forcefully deprive us of fundamental habits. Loosening the hardened soil of our routine behaviour and thoughts will have an enlivening effect on our vital energy, our mental vigour and our power of imagination. But what is most important, into that loosened soil we shall be able to plant the seeds of vigorous spiritual progress.

Associative Thought

Mental habituation to standard reactions, to sequences of activity and to judgements of people or things proceeds by way of associative thinking. From the objects, ideas, situations and people that we encounter, we select certain distinctive marks, and associate these marks with our own response to them. If these encounters recur, they are associated first with those marks selected earlier, and then with our original, or strongest response. Thus these marks become a signal for releasing a standard reaction, which may consist of a long sequence of connected acts or thoughts familiar through repeated practice or experience. This way of functioning makes it unnecessary for us to apply new effort and painstaking scrutiny to each single step in such a sequence. The result is a great simplification of life, permitting us to release energy for other tasks. In fact, in the evolution of the human mind, associative thinking was a progressive step of decisive importance. It enabled us to learn from experience, and thus led up to the discovery and application of causal laws.

Yet along with these benefits, associative thinking can also bring many grave dangers if it is applied faultily or thoughtlessly and not carefully controlled. Let us draw up a partial list of these danger points:

1. Associative thinking, recurring again and again in similar situations, may easily perpetuate and strengthen faulty or incomplete initial observations, errors of judgement and emotional prejudices such as love, hate and pride.

2. Incomplete observations and restricted viewpoints in judgement, sufficient to deal with one particular situation, may prove quite inadequate and entail grave consequences if mechanically applied to changed circumstances.

3. Due to misdirected associative thinking, a strong instinctive dislike may be felt for things, places or people which in some way are merely reminiscent of unpleasant experiences, but actually have no connection with them.

These briefly stated instances show how vital it is for us to scrutinize from time to time the mental grooves of our associative thoughts, and to review the various habits and stereotype reactions deriving from them. In other words, we must step out of our ruts, regain a direct vision of things and make a fresh appraisal of our habits in the light of that vision.

If we look once again over the list of potential dangers deriving from uncontrolled associative thinking, we shall better understand the Buddha's insistence upon getting to the bedrock of experience. In the profound and terse stanzas called "The Cave," included in the Suttanipāta, the Buddha says that the "full penetration of *sense impression* (*phassa*) will make one free from greed" and that "by understanding *perception* (*saññā*), one will be able to cross the flood of saṃsāra" (vv. 778ff.).[1] By placing mindfulness as a guard at the very first gate through which thoughts enter the mind, we shall be able to control the incomers much more easily, and shut out unwanted intruders. Thus the purity of "luminous consciousness" can be maintained against "adventitious defilements" (AN 1:51).

The *Satipaṭṭhāna Sutta* provides a systematic training for inducing direct, fresh and undistorted vision. The training covers the entire personality in its physical and mental aspects, and includes the whole world of experience. The methodical application of the several exercises to oneself (*ajjhatta*), to others (*bahiddhā*) and alternatingly to both will help uncover erroneous conceptions due to misdirected associative thinking and misapplied analogies.

The principal types of false associative thinking are covered, in the terminology of the Dhamma, by the four kinds of *misapprehension or perverted views* (*vipallāsa*), i.e., wrongly taking (1) what is impermanent for permanent, (2) what is painful, or conducive to pain, for happiness, (3) what has no self and is unsubstantial for a self or an abiding substance, and (4) what is impure for beautiful. These perverted views arise through a false apprehension of the characteristic marks of things. Under the influence of our

---

1. Compare also the passage on the significance of sense impression (or contact) in the concluding sections of the *Brahmajāla Sutta* (DN 1).

passions and false theories, we perceive things selectively in a one-sided or erroneous way, and then associate them wrongly with other ideas. By applying bare attention to our perceptions and impressions, gradually we can free them from these misapprehensions, progressing steadily towards the *direct vision* of things as they really are.

The Sense of Urgency

One who has clear and direct vision, stirred to a sense of urgency (*saṃvega*) by things that are deeply moving, will experience a release of energy and courage enabling him to break through his timid hesitations and his rigid routine of life and thought. If that sense of urgency is kept alive, it will bestow the earnestness and persistence required for the work of liberation. Thus said the teachers of old:

> This very world here is our field of action.
> It harbours the unfoldment of the holy path,
> And many things to break complacency.
> Be stirred by things which may well move the heart,
> And being stirred, strive wisely and fight on!

Our closest surroundings are full of stirring things. If we generally do not perceive them as such, that is because habit has made our vision dull and our heart insensitive.

The same thing happens to us even with the Buddha's teaching. When we first encounter the teaching, we receive a powerful intellectual and emotional stimulation; but gradually the impetus tends to lose its original freshness and impelling force. The remedy is to constantly renew it by turning to the fullness of life around us, which illustrates the Four Noble Truths in ever new variations. A direct vision will impart new lifeblood even to the most common experiences of every day, so that their true nature appears through the dim haze of habit and speaks to us with a fresh voice. It may well be just the long accustomed sight of the beggar at the street corner, of a weeping child or the illness of a friend which startles us afresh, makes us think and stirs our sense of urgency in treading resolutely the path that leads to the cessation of suffering.

We know the beautiful account of how Prince Siddhattha first came face to face with old age, illness and death while driving his chariot through the royal city after a long period of isolation in a make-believe world. This ancient story may well be historical fact, for we know that in the lives of many great men common events often gain a symbolic significance and lead to major consequences far beyond their ordinary appearance. Great minds find significance in the seemingly commonplace and invest the fleeting moment with far-reaching efficacy. But, without contesting the inner truth of that old story, we may reasonably believe that the young prince had actually seen before, with his fleshy eyes, old people, sick people and those who had succumbed to death. However, on all these earlier occasions, he would not have been touched very deeply by these sights—as is the case with most of us most of the time. That earlier lack of sensitivity may have been due to the carefully protected, artificial seclusion of his petty, though princely, happiness—the hereditary routine of his life into which his father had placed him. Only when he broke through that golden cage of easy-going habits could the facts of suffering strike him as forcibly as if he had seen them for the first time. Then only was he stirred by them to a sense of urgency that led him out of the home life and set his feet firmly on the road to enlightenment.

The more *clearly* and *deeply* our minds and hearts respond to the truth of suffering manifest in the very common facts of our existence, the less often shall we need a repetition of the lesson and the shorter will be our migration through saṃsāra. The *clarity* of perception evoking our response will come from an undeflected directness of vision, bestowed by bare attention (*sati*); and the *depth* of experience will come from wise reflection or clear comprehension (*sampajañña*).

The Road to Insight

Directness of vision is also a chief characteristic of the methodical practice of insight meditation. There it is identified with the direct or experiential knowledge bestowed by meditation, as distinguished from the inferential knowledge obtained by study and reflection. In the meditative development of insight, one's own physical and mental processes are directly viewed, without the interference of abstract concepts or the filtering screens of emotional evaluation. For in this context these only obscure or camouflage the naked facts, detracting from the strong immediate impact of reality. Conceptual generalizations from experience are very useful in their place; but if they interrupt the meditative practice of bare attention, they tend to "shove aside" or dispose of the particular fact, by saying, as it were: "It is nothing else but this." Generalizing thought inclines to become impatient with a recurrent type, and after having it classified, soon finds it boring.

Bare attention, however, being the key instrument of methodical insight, keeps to the particular. It follows keenly the rise and fall of successive physical and mental processes. Though all phenomena of a given series may be true to type (e.g., inhalations and exhalations), bare attention regards each of them as distinct, and conscientiously registers its separate birth and death. If mindfulness remains alert, these repetitions of type will, by their multiplication, exert not a reduced but an intensified impact on the mind. The three characteristics— impermanence, suffering and voidness of self—inherent in the process observed, will stand out more and more clearly. They will appear in the light shed by the phenomena themselves, not in a *borrowed* light; not even a light borrowed from the Buddha, the peerless and indispensable guide to these experiences. These physical and mental phenomena, in their "self-luminosity," will then convey a growing sense of urgency to the meditator: revulsion, dissatisfaction and awareness of danger, followed by detachment—though certainly, joy, happiness and calm, too, will not be absent throughout the practice. Then, if all other conditions of inner maturity are fulfilled, the first direct vision of final liberation will dawn with the stream-winner's (*sotāpanna*) indubitable knowledge: "Whatever has the nature of arising, has the nature of vanishing."

Thus, in the unfoldment of the power of mindfulness, Satipaṭṭhāna will prove itself as the true embodiment of the Dhamma, of which it was said:

"Well-proclaimed is the Dhamma by the Blessed One, visible here and now, not delayed, inviting inspection, onward-leading, to be directly experienced by the wise."

—§§§—

THE BUDDHIST PUBLICATION SOCIETY

The BPS is an approved charity dedicated to making known the Teaching of the Buddha, which has a vital message for all people. Founded in 1958, the BPS has published a wide variety of books and booklets covering a great range of topics. Its publications include accurate annotated translations of the Buddha's discourses, standard reference works, as well as original contemporary expositions of Buddhist thought and practice. These works present Buddhism as it truly is—a dynamic force which has influenced receptive minds for the past 2500 years and is still as relevant today as it was when it first arose. For more information about the BPS and our publications, please visit our website, or contact:

Administrative Secretary
Buddhist Publication Society
P.O. Box 61
54 Sangharaja Mawatha
Kandy • Sri Lanka

E-mail: bps@bps.lk
web site: http://www.bps.lk
Tel: 0094 81 223 7283 • Fax: 0094 81 222 3679